CREATURES ALL AROUND US

Insects
in the Garden

by D. M. Souza

Carolrhoda Books, Inc./Minneapolis

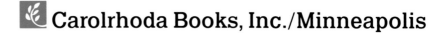

Many of the photos in this book show the insects larger than life size. The degree of magnification varies.

Library of Congress Cataloging-in-Publication Data

Souza, D. M. (Dorothy M.)
  Insects in the garden / by D. M. Souza.
    p.   cm.
  Includes index.
  Summary: Describes the life cycle and habits of various insects found in the common garden.
  ISBN 0-87614-439-3
  1. Insects—Juvenile literature. 2. Insect pests—Juvenile literature. 3. Beneficial insects—Juvenile literature. 4. Garden fauna—Juvenile literature. [1. Insects. 2. Garden animals.] I. Title.
QL467.2.S68 1991
595.7—dc20   90-38292
                                  CIP
                                    AC

A bumblebee pollinating a flower is a familiar sight in the garden.

Insects in the Garden

Step into the garden and notice the apples, pears, plums, cherries, and nuts growing on the trees. You may also find melons, pumpkins, or juicy berries on vines and shrubs. Surprising as it may seem, insects play a large part in bringing all of these delicious things to life.

Before any fruit grows on a tree or plant, a flower must bloom and produce seeds. Seeds develop when the flower's pollen (the male cells) reaches the stigma (the female part of the flower). This is where insects come in. They act as pollen carriers, or **pollinators**.

3

The yucca moth has a special relationship with the yucca plant.

When an insect lands on a plant and begins sipping nectar, it picks up bits of pollen on its legs or body. Then it moves to other flowers, and some of the pollen is rubbed onto the stigmas of those flowers.

Bees are perhaps the best known pollinators, but other insects such as butterflies, moths, and even flies carry pollen too. The Smyrna fig, for example, depends on the chalcid, or fig wasp, to pollinate it. A small white moth known as the yucca moth has a special relationship with the yucca plant. Not only does this moth pollinate the plant, but the female lays her eggs deep inside its flowers. When the **larvae** (LAR-vee), or young, hatch, they feed on the seeds. Thanks to the moth, there are enough seeds to satisfy the hungry larvae and to produce more yucca plants.

4

The insects in the garden also work as scavengers—that is, they feed on dead things. Imagine the lifeless body of a mouse lying under a bush. Several burying beetles catch its scent and fly to the scene. They dig away the earth under the dead mouse until its body sinks below the surface. Then they cover it with dirt. Female burying beetles lay their eggs close by, and when the young hatch, they have a large supply of meat to eat. Soon they grow up and bury other dead creatures lying in the garden.

It's true, some insects are pests and damage plants by chewing, sucking, or boring holes in leaves, stems, and bark. However, other insects that are **predators** (PREH-duh-terz) feed on these pests and help control the amount of damage they do. Dragonflies and damselflies are both predators, as are some flies and beetles.

Tiger beetles, like many other animals, are predators that feed on other insects.

5

This froghopper nymph is hiding in white foam that it has released from its body.

There is a constant battle going on between predators and their prey. To escape being caught, some insects "play dead." Inchworms, for example, hold out their bodies like twigs, while flea beetles fold up their legs and fall to the ground. Other insects **camouflage** (KAM-oh-flazh) themselves. The larvae of tortoise beetles gather debris and carry it over their bodies like an umbrella. Young froghopper **nymphs** surround themselves with a sudsy white blob that they release from their bodies. They hide under this blob day and night.

Yes, a garden is an exciting place. There are many things to taste, see, touch, and hear. If you move quietly and look carefully, you may make some strange, interesting, and amusing discoveries.

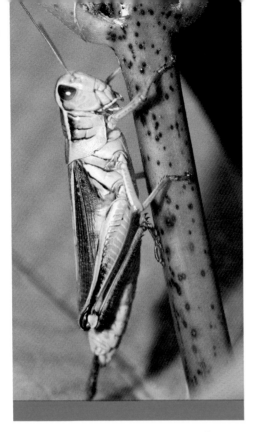

The grasshopper is a talented jumper.

High Jumpers

A black-and-white cat sits motionless on a pathway. Its eyes are focused on an insect inches away. The insect jumps, the cat leaps, and the chase is on.

Minutes later the cat returns without its catch. The insect it has been chasing is a grasshopper, one of the best jumpers and escape artists in the insect world. If it were as big as a kangaroo, it could leap farther than the length of two football fields. In an Insect Olympics, it would win a gold medal. No wonder the cat couldn't catch it!

The grasshopper and the cat are not at all alike. First, the grasshopper has five eyes: a large one on either side of its head, one in the middle of its forehead, and two others behind its antennae. Second, its ears are not on its head but near the front of its **abdomen**, the third section of its body. Some grasshoppers even have their ears on their legs, just below their knees. Instead of a nose, the grasshopper has several small openings, or **spiracles** (SPIHR-uh-kuhlz), on its side. It breathes through its spiracles.

You can see three of this grasshopper's five eyes. The other two are behind its antennae.

This young grasshopper nymph looks like a smaller version of an adult grasshopper, but it has no wings.

To lay her eggs, a female grasshopper makes a hole in the ground with a long part of her abdomen known as the **ovipositor** (oh-vih-PAH-zih-tuhr). After releasing her eggs into the hole, she covers them with a pastelike liquid that protects them during the winter.

Unlike many other insects, grasshoppers do not go through **complete metamorphosis**, or four stages of development. Instead, the young nymphs hatch looking very much like their parents. They are smaller, however, and wingless.

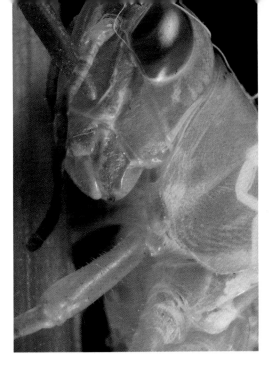

At first glance, this may look like a grass-hopper, but it's actually a recently shed grasshopper skin.

Grasshopper nymphs have big appetites and immediately begin eating plant leaves and juicy stems with their scissor-like mouthparts. Their bodies grow quickly, so quickly that their outer coverings, or **cuticles** (KYOO-tih-kuhlz), cannot hold them for long. Every few days grasshopper nymphs **molt**—they burst out of their skins and leave the old ones hanging on plants or fences. You may spot one of these empty skins lying somewhere in the garden. Nymphs continue growing for 40 to 60 days until they finally become adults. This way of developing is known as **incomplete metamorphosis**.

Many grasshoppers, along with their cricket and katydid relatives, grow up to be very musical. They make music by rubbing one part of their bodies against another. Long-horned grasshoppers rub the sharp edge of one wing (called a scraper) against a filelike ridge on the other wing. The band-winged grasshopper snaps its wings together while flying, and the slant-faced grasshopper rubs its hind legs across its front wings. Most of these music makers are males trying to attract a mate. Some can be heard playing day or night. Have you heard them?

Long-horned grass-hoppers such as this one make music by rubbing their wings against each other.

All grasshoppers chew on plants, and if there are only one or two in the garden, they do not do too much damage. However, large swarms of grasshoppers have destroyed entire fields of corn or other food crops in many places around the world. These swarming grasshoppers are called locusts.

Some people have discovered that grasshoppers are good to eat. They roast the insects or add them to soups and stews. That black-and-white cat in the garden is not the only one that enjoys catching grasshoppers!

One grasshopper won't do much damage in a garden, but large swarms of them can be very destructive.

A mantid egg case hanging from a branch.

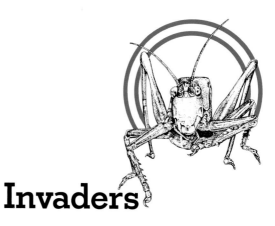

Invaders

Hanging from a low branch in a peach tree is an odd-looking object. It is grayish brown and about the size and shape of a walnut. This is the egg case of a mantid, and if we move closer, we will see something amazing happening.

Hundreds of insects, so small that they are almost invisible, are spilling out of the case and running over the garden like tiny invaders from another planet.

These creatures are newborn mantid nymphs, and they look like miniature versions of their parents. They have tremendous appetites and gobble up plant lice and other small insects they find.

Within a short time, they increase in size and turn darker in color. Most mantids are greenish brown. Gradually the young begin to hunt for larger insects, such as flies, crickets, beetles, roaches, bumblebees, and sometimes even other mantids. Some have even been known to attack birds, mice, or snakes. They are absolutely fearless.

After mantids become adults, they are somewhat lazy. Rather than hunt, they sit motionless on a branch or leaf and wait for a meal to come to them. They hold their two long, spiked front legs, or forelegs, in front of their heads. Unlike other insects, mantids frequently turn their heads almost completely around to watch for approaching prey.

*This mantid is in the
praying position,
waiting for its prey.*

As soon as another insect comes close, a mantid's forelegs shoot out toward it. One lower leg closes, knifelike, against the upper one and holds the victim in place. Then the mantid's strong cutting jaws bite down on it.

Nothing appears to be too hard for mantids to eat, and nothing upsets their stomachs. They can eat the body of a deadly black widow, the sharp hairs of a caterpillar, or the hard covering of a beetle—and still be hungry.

After eating, mantids spend their time washing their faces, much as a cat does. Then they sit back, lift their forelegs, and wait for the next meal to arrive. Because of the way they hold up their forelegs, they are sometimes called "praying mantises."

17

During late summer and fall, female mantids lay several hundred eggs and attach them to twigs, branches, or blades of grass. They cover their eggs with a foamy substance that hardens soon after it is touched by air. It becomes a protective case for the eggs during the wet and cold winter months.

18

When spring comes again, and the sun begins to warm the earth, young mantid nymphs crawl out of their egg cases and scatter throughout the garden. If you come upon a large insect sitting motionless on a plant, move closer. If it looks back at you with big, bulging eyes, you'll know that one of those young mantids has grown up.

Have you ever seen a mantid staring at you with its big, bulging eyes?

These dragonflies are taking a rare break from flying.

Dragons in the Sky

Hundreds of mosquitoes are buzzing around a small pond in the garden. Suddenly a large insect shaped like an airplane appears overhead. Its long wings beat so rapidly (about 1,600 times a minute) that they hardly seem to move. Sunlight falls on the insect's wings, and the colors of the rainbow are reflected. This is the most amazing flier in the insect world—the dragonfly.

Left: *Dragonflies see very well with their large compound eyes.*

Right: *Dragonflies have four thin, gauzy wings.*

Large compound eyes spot the mosquitoes, and the dragonfly swoops down. Six long legs reach out and form a kind of basket around some of the mosquitoes. Then two forelegs carry the captured victims to the insect's mouth. Again and again this happens, and the dragonfly rarely lands to rest.

Dragonflies are powerful insects with wingspans that sometimes measure 2 to 3 inches. When they first appeared on earth more than 300 million years ago, their wings stretched 2 feet from tip to tip. Dragonflies' four wings are thin and gauzy and are supported by a framework of tiny veins. In some species these wings are brightly colored and patterned with bars of blue, green, red, yellow, black, or brown.

Damselflies are closely related to dragonflies and are sometimes mistaken for them. Damselflies are not, however, as large or as powerful as dragonflies. Their back wings are narrower and are held over their bodies when they are at rest, rather than straight out, as dragonflies' are. Another difference is that damselflies lay their eggs in the stems of plants, while dragonflies lay their eggs in water.

Damselflies are smaller than dragonflies, and they hold their wings over their bodies.

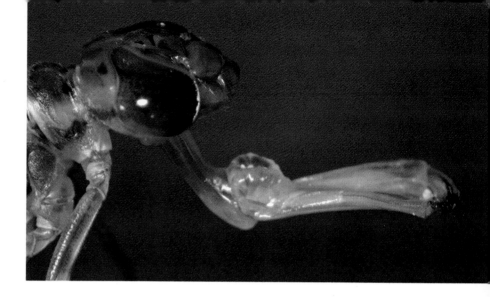

This dragonfly nymph has pushed its labium forward to catch its prey.

When female dragonflies are ready to lay their eggs, they fly close to the surface of a pond or stream and dip their ovipositors into the water. Some females cover their eggs with a jellylike substance that helps the eggs stick to water plants instead of floating downstream.

When dragonfly nymphs hatch, they do not look like their parents and are really quite ugly. Each one has an underlip, called a **labium** (LAY-bee-uhm), that is half as long as the rest of its body. Most of the time, it is folded over the nymph's face and looks like a mask. When water insects, tadpoles, or even small fish come near, the lip is thrust forward, grips the victim, and drags it back to the nymph's mouth. Then the labium is folded back over the nymph's face.

Nymphs live in water for as little as a month to as long as five years, depending upon their **species** (SPEE-sheez), or kind. They breathe by means of gills found inside their bodies near the end of their abdomens. If something frightens them, they shoot out a stream of water behind them and move forward like rockets. At other times, they crawl around on their six legs.

As nymphs change in size and shape, they molt. Before the last molt, they slowly crawl up the stem of a weed or plant in the pond. The size of their bodies forces their cuticles to slowly split down the back and across the head. As the split widens, adult dragonflies wiggle out. Their bodies are now very soft and wet, and their wings and legs are weak. They must wait without moving for an hour or more until their body parts dry and harden. Then the beautiful insects take to the air.

They can zoom straight up like an arrow, hover like a helicopter, whizz backward or forward, and land as gracefully as a feather. So amazing are dragonflies in the air that scientists study them to discover the secrets of their flight maneuvers. One day we may have planes that are faster and quieter and can land on very small spaces, thanks to dragonflies.

Dragonflies are gifted fliers. They can also be quite beautiful.

These Polistes *wasps are gathered on their nest.*

Builders

The sight and sound of a wasp buzzing around your head may send you running, but stay and watch these insects closely for a while, and you'll discover how clever they are.

If they fly back and forth to a small gray structure hanging in a tree or under a leaf, they are probably wasps of the *Polistes* (poh-LIH-steez) group. The word means "founder of a city," and that is what *Polistes* wasps do— they build colonies of wasps.

This Polistes *queen is adding wood pulp to her nest.*

The gray structure consists of several six-sided **cells** with their openings facing downward. They look somewhat like the wax cells of honeybees' hives but are made of a material similar to papier-mâché. Female wasps chew and rechew bits of leaves, pieces of rotted wood, or dead plant stems and mix these with saliva until they become pulpy masses. Then they shape these masses into cells.

After making several cells, these wasps, called queens, lay long white eggs, one in each cell. These eggs hatch into white larvae and hang head down in their cells. Their bodies give off a sticky substance that holds them in place and keeps them from falling.

Polistes queens then become hunters and search for insects, which they chew into morsels like hamburger patties for their young. *Polistes* larvae molt several times. As soon as they are big enough to fill up their cells, they spin a cap of silk over themselves and turn into **pupae** (PYOO-pee).

It takes about 48 days for *Polistes* wasps to develop from eggs into adults. The first wasps to come out of the pupal stage are workers, who take over the building of the colony. While queens lay more eggs, workers hunt for building material, enlarge the nest, and gather food.

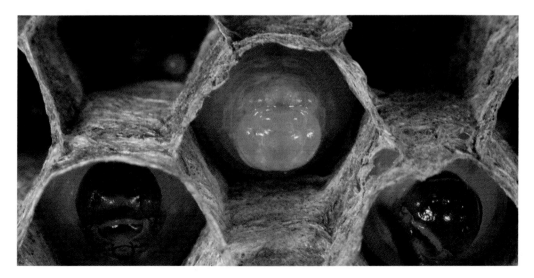

The Polistes *larva in the middle cell is molting.*

Hornets, like Polistes *wasps, are clever builders. Have you ever seen a hornet nest?*

Colonies then grow in size and number until there may be as many as one hundred six-sided cells. Male wasps with white faces come from some of the last cells. Also hatching are young queens who will mate with them. When cold weather arrives, these queens will find a protected place to hide. They are the only *Polistes* wasps that survive the winter. The following spring they will begin building new colonies.

Another type of wasp you are likely to spot in the garden is the mud wasp or mud dauber. These solitary insects do not live in colonies, but they are just as clever as their social relatives. Female mud daubers collect mud and shape it into little balls with their **mandibles** (MAN-dih-buhlz), or jaws, and front feet. Then they fly off with these balls to places they have chosen as building sites. These may be rocks, boards, or any hard surface protected from the rain. Here they spread the mud balls and begin shaping them. Dozens of times they fly off to gather more building material, until the structure grows from a single room measuring about 1 inch deep to an apartment of 8 or even 16 rooms. Each nest is stocked with six or seven paralyzed spiders that the wasps have caught. Then the wasps lay eggs and seal each room with more mud.

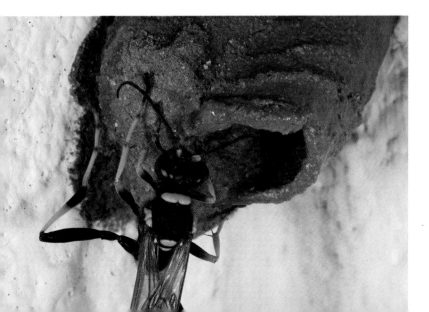

This female mud dauber is building her nest.

33

When mud dauber larvae hatch, they have enough spider meals to last them through the winter. They grow in much the same way as the larvae of the *Polistes* wasps. No workers hatch, however, because mud daubers are solitary rather than social wasps. When spring returns, young wasps chew their way out of their mud apartments, and the garden is once again filled with clever builders.

The mud dauber larvae in this nest have plenty of spider meals to eat.

Earwigs may squirt a foul-smelling liquid if threatened.

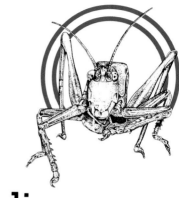

In Hiding

Some insects are not as easy to find as the ones we've just seen. You may have to do a bit of detective work to uncover them.

Earwigs love to hide under boards, rocks, or piles of leaves, so try searching in those places. These small, brown insects have large, clawlike structures called pincers on the ends of their bodies that they use for defense. Some even squirt a foul-smelling liquid when frightened, so step aside! At night, they come out to feed on plants, slow-moving snails, insect larvae, and their own dead.

*The light green
patch on this leaf
is actually an insect
called a leafhopper.*

Brown leaves on some plants may signal that leafhoppers are close by. These insects are only ⅛ to ¼ inch long, and under a powerful microscope, their bristlelike antennae and patches of color make them look as if they are wearing glasses and have funny caps on their heads. Most leafhoppers are yellow, yellow green, or white, but others are multicolored. One type of leafhopper even has red, white, and blue stripes on its back.

Young bean plants that have been cut down overnight are a sign that a cutworm has been at work. Cutworms are not worms at all but the larvae of owl moths. Dig around beneath the plant and you may discover a grayish caterpillar. This is a cutworm.

If you spot a twig moving, don't be surprised. It's probably an insect called a walking stick. These relatives of the grasshopper are long, thin, and wingless and actually look like sticks.

Take a closer peek at the bark of a tree. You may find a well-camouflaged moth clinging to it and blending in with the bark.

As you move in and around the garden searching for signs of insects, be alert. Many insects in hiding are probably keeping their eyes on you!

You can hardly tell the difference between this walking stick and the twig above it.

Scientists who study animals group them together according to their similarities and differences. Animals that have certain features in common are placed in the same **order**. For example, insects in the same order may go through similar stages before they reach adulthood, or they may have the same kind of mouthparts or the same number of wings. There are about 25 orders of insects in all. The orders of some of the insects discussed in this book are described below.

ORDER	MEANING	EXAMPLES	TYPE OF MOUTHPARTS	NUMBER OF WINGS	WHERE USUALLY FOUND
Dermaptera	skin wings	earwigs	chewing	4	everywhere
Homoptera	uniform wings	leafhoppers, spittlebugs	chewing	4	in debris, under rocks and bark
Hymenoptera	membrane wings	wasps, bees	chewing, chewing-sucking, or lapping	4	in ground, on plants and flowers
Odonata	with teeth	dragonflies, damselflies	chewing	4	young: in water adults: near water
Orthoptera	straight wings	cockroaches, grasshoppers, mantids	chewing	4	on plants, in ground, and in houses

Glossary

abdomen: the back section of an insect's body

camouflage: a way animals hide themselves by blending in with their environments

cells: sections of nests built by wasps and bees

complete metamorphosis: a way of growing in which an insect goes from egg to larva to pupa to adult

cuticles: the outer skins or coverings of some insects

incomplete metamorphosis: a way of growing in which an insect goes from egg to nymph to adult

labium: the lip of certain insects, such as dragonflies

larvae: the young of some insects

mandibles: mouthparts that some insects use to chew

molt: to shed an outer skin or cuticle

nymphs: the young of insects that go through incomplete metamorphosis

order: a group of animals with a number of features in common

ovipositor: a structure through which many female insects lay eggs

pollinators: insects that carry pollen to flowers

predators: animals that kill other animals for food

pupae: insects in the pupal stage, the last stage of growth before adulthood

species: type of animal

spiracles: breathing holes on the bodies of some insects

Index

The photographs are reproduced through the courtesy of: pp. 3, 7, 11, 13, 22, 29, © Gerry Lemmo; pp. 4, 5, 6, 33, 34, 37, © Robert and Linda Mitchell; pp. 8, 15, 18, 25, 35, Dwight R. Kuhn; pp. 9, 10, 30, 31, front cover (both), back cover, Donald L. Rubbelke; pp. 12, 24, 27, 28, 36, © Frank Stibritz; pp. 16, 32, © John Serrao; p. 20, © Mary Stibritz; pp. 21, 23, © Gregory K. Scott.